Management: Take Charge of Your Team

Communication, Leadership, Coaching and Conflict Resolution

2nd Edition

By
ALAN ANDERSON

Alan Anderson

Management: Take Charge of Your Team

© Copyright 2015 by Alan Anderson - All rights reserved.

In no way is it legal to reproduce, duplicate, or transmit any part of this document in either electronic means or in printed format. Recording of this publication is strictly prohibited and any storage of this document is not allowed unless with written permission from the publisher. All rights reserved.

The information provided herein is stated to be truthful and consistent, in that any liability, in terms of inattention or otherwise, by any usage or abuse of any policies, processes, or directions contained within is the solitary and utter responsibility of the recipient reader. Under no circumstances will any legal responsibility or blame be held against the publisher for any reparation, damages, or monetary loss due to the information herein, either directly or indirectly.

Respective authors own all copyrights not held by the publisher.

Legal Notice:
This book is copyright protected. This is only for personal use. You cannot amend, distribute, sell, use, quote or paraphrase any part or the content within this book without the consent of the author or copyright owner. Legal action will be pursued if this is breached.

Disclaimer Notice:
Please note the information contained within this document is for educational and entertainment purposes only. Every attempt has been made to provide accurate, up to date and reliable complete information. No warranties of any kind are expressed or implied. Readers acknowledge that the author is not engaging in the rendering of legal, financial, medical or professional advice.
By reading this document, the reader agrees that under no circumstances are we responsible for any losses, direct or

Alan Anderson

indirect, which are incurred as a result of the use of information contained within this document, including, but not limited to, — errors, omissions, or inaccuracies

Table of Contents

INTRODUCTION..7

CHAPTER 1 – LEADERSHIP AND MANAGEMENT...................9
    What Makes For Great Leaders?......................................11
    Approaches To Leadership...12

CHAPTER 2 – TRAITS LEADERSHIP APPROACH....................15

CHAPTER 3 – BEHAVIORAL LEADERSHIP APPROACH.........17
    Center Of Attention..17
    Relationships..18
    The Grid..18

CHAPTER 4 – SITUATIONAL LEADERSHIP APPROACH.......21
    Situation Leadership Models...22

CHAPTER 5 – SUBORDINATES' PERPECTIVE MODELS........31

CHAPTER 6 – LEADERSHIP ALTERNATIVES AND NEUTRALIZERS..33

CHAPTER 7 – MANAGEMENT...35
    Managing Effective Teams: What To Avoid.................38
    General Strategies For Managing A Winning Team........42

CHAPTER 8 – LEARNING ABOUT YOUR TEAM.....................45
    Getting to know your team's strengths and weaknesses..45
    Dealing with deadlines and check points........................46

CHAPTER 9 – GROOMING TEAM MEMBERS AND DEVELOPING SKILLS..49
    Identify The Weakest Links...49
    Deciding Optimally For Weak Links...............................50
    Choose The Optimal Strategy..51

CHAPTER 10 – YOUR COACHING SKILLS..............................53
    Improving your coaching skills.......................................53

CHAPTER 11 – COMMUNICATION..57
    How entrepreneurs communicate with a team................57
    Learn to communicate your objective clearly...................58

CHAPTER 12 – LEARNING THE ART OF ALLOCATION/DELEGATION...61
    Delegation directions...62
    The Reason you need to Learn Delegation........................62
    Delegating with clear instructions....................................63
    Investment...64

CHAPTER 13 – TEAM INCENTIVES..67
    So how can you make projects more competitive?..........67

CHAPTER 14 – LEARNING CONFLICT RESOLUTION.............71

CHAPTER 15 – SHIFTING DEADLINES OR CHANGED PROJECTIONS...75
    Holding a meeting to announce changes.......................76

CHAPTER 16 – REPORTING OF PROBLEMS..........................79
    Making your team aware..80

CHAPTER 17: CRISES AND HOW TO MANAGE THEM EFFICIENTLY..83

CONCLUSION..93

Introduction

It's always a little frightening being put in charge of a team for the first time, but once you get the hang of the basic principles, it actually becomes second nature. I remember being asked to lead a team of very hostile workers. Why were they hostile? The fact was that each of the team had their own agendas and each thought that they were actually too experienced to be led by someone that had so little experience within their company.

What transpired was that I had to prove myself in many ways and it is this experience that I am bringing to the table today. If you are afraid of leadership and have never led a team before, you have come to the right place. Knowing people as well as I do, I have devised a system that is fail-safe. It works with whatever kind of team you head because it uses basic principles that have been proven time and again to work. The book is split into different sections so that you can pick and choose your subject or your own weakness and work on it. These weaknesses will go away, but they really do need you to learn what it is that you're afraid of and how to handle it and that's where my years of experience will help you.

Does it hold the answers to most situations you may be faced with? I'd like to think it does because it's gleaned from over 30 years of running teams in different kinds of industry and deals with all the character types that you are likely to run into. Never think that anyone within the team is a weak link or you lose your leadership respect. Remember, even those with weak skills will have a place on the team and can be used for the more mundane aspects that other people don't enjoy. This book will show you how to sort out who is who and to use them to the best of your ability. It will also show you how to sort out disputes among team members. Your leadership example is of paramount importance and you need to win the respect of your team in order to be able to sort out problems as and when they happen.

The idea behind writing this book was to use my experience to help those starting out and to be able to give useful and sound advice. There are many corporate books on leadership. What makes mine different is that it's written by someone who has been where you are currently standing, and who understands your difficulty with being faced with the job of team leader for the first time. Walk through the pages and learn how it's done. It's actually easier than you may imagine, once you know what it is that you need to be doing.

Chapter 1 – Leadership And Management

Leadership and management are two related topics that are separated only by a really fine line. Frequently though, that line becomes blurred resulting in confusing one for the other. On the other hand, there are also many different views about which between the two is more important. With all honesty, both management and leadership are important – they go hand-in-hand, so to speak. If you'd like take effective charge of your own team, you'll need both leadership and management to complement with each other.

Management and leadership have been compared in more than a few occasions with the hope of clearly distinguishing one from the other. Simply put, leadership is doing the right things and management, according to legendary business guru Peter Drucker, is doing things right. Leadership is about leaning a ladder on the correct wall and management is effectively being able to climb that ladder of success, per another well-renowned guru, Stephen Covey. He also adds that leadership means getting priorities in order – doing first things first – and management means being disciplined enough to carry those priorities out. Personally, I define leadership as being able to set the direction and getting others on board while management is navigating the team towards getting there.

In his famous book A Force Of Change: How Leadership Differs From Management (1990), John P. Kotter compared in detail management and leadership, specifically in 4 important areas of business: agenda, network development, execution and results.

In terms of making your team's agenda, management will focus on budgeting and planning. As a manager, you'll identify particular steps and timelines for achieving significant results as well as allocating the needed resources for successfully achieving them. As a leader, you'll focus on the direction setting part like creating your team or organization's vision as well as laying down the general strategies for achieving particular results required for achieving that vision.

In terms of the second area, which is network development or creating the necessary structures or network for achieving your team's agenda, you as a manager will need to create the organizational structure that will optimize your team's chances of meeting requirements, fill up such structure with the right people, delegate authority and responsibilities to those people, come up with the necessary procedures and policies that will guide your members towards the team's successfully achievement of the agenda and create a way to monitor progress and implementation. As a leader, you'll need to be able to communicate all necessary information and direction to the right people concerned.

The third area according to Kotter is execution. As a manager, you're responsible for controlling the way the plans are executed by your team, including management of any diversion from such plans. You'll need to monitor things as they happen – according to plan – and act to correct any deviations promptly. As a leader, your concern is to inspire and motivate your team members, especially when the going gets rough, which may increase the team's risk of not being able to successfully achieve the agenda or goals. Some of the ways you'll be able to do this is through addressing your team's personal needs for such things as affirmation and validation, among other things.

In terms of results, your job as a manager is to ensure predictability and order that will help your team to achieve the necessary results expected of it. As a leader, you may need to change things up every now and then to ensure your team's effectiveness.

It's preposterous to think that you can lead well without managing well. The same goes for the belief that you can manage well without having to be a good leader. Together they stand but divided, they'll fall. For effectively and successfully leading or managing your team, you'll also need to be a good leader.

One good definition of leadership is one from the Search Inside Yourself Leadership Institute, which says leadership is the art of leading people to purposefully achieve results that couldn't have been achieved otherwise. Great leadership doesn't accidentally produce results – it does so deliberately. Great leadership can make a mediocre team into a great one, a failing team into one that's very successful and a team that's at the bottom of the productivity ladder into one that's on top. If you want to manage your team effectively, you also need to lead them well.

What Makes For Great Leaders?

One of the things that can make you a great leader is self-awareness, which means your very much in touch and know your current emotional state. It also means knowing your weaknesses and strengths, when you're hitting your groove or when you seem to be out of whack. Most of all, you need to know your limits. Don't go for the lie that we are all limitless and that the only limits we have are what we think they are.

Another think that will make you into a great leader is self-direction. This means you know what necessary steps to take and more importantly, can take those steps with conviction. When you're like that, you don't procrastinate, you organize things well and ultimately get things done. As mentioned, you need to be convinced that the steps you're taking are the best so you can decide and act quickly, particularly during moments where you don't have the luxury of being able to do a SWOT analysis over lunch. There are just days that you'll need to decide on the run and if great leaders are able to do that when needed.

As a great leader, you'll need to be a visionary, i.e., begin with the end in mind as Stephen Covey used to say. This means you know the end result you want your team to achieve and because of that, you and your team can focus only on those things that are necessary for success. You'll be able to rally your team towards a much greater goal than their personal ones.

If you want to be a great leader, you need to be able to motivate people well. If you're able to do that, you don't merely tell your members what needs to be done – you also make them want to do them! Believe me, there's nothing much better than having team members who want to do things for the team to succeed. As a leader, you should primarily use influence instead of authority, the latter for use only on rainy days.

The last characteristic you'll need to develop to be a great leader is emotional intelligence or EQ. This is because people who have high EQ tend to be more self-aware, more in touch with people and have a great ability to control themselves. These characteristics are without a doubt very important to be a great leader.

Approaches To Leadership

Exercising leadership isn't just about having the characteristics I enumerated above – it also requires wisdom or strategies in using such characteristics to effectively lead your people for effective management of your team. These strategies or approaches include:

- The Traits Leadership Approach;
- The Behavioral Leadership Approach;
- The Situational Leadership Approach;
- The Subordinates' Perspective Approach; and

- Leadership Substitute Approaches.

From Chapters 2 to 6, we'll take a look at these leadership approaches that will help you establish a great foundation for implementing the management techniques in the remaining chapters. Next up, the Traits Leadership Approach.

Alan Anderson

Chapter 2 – Traits Leadership Approach

Names like Abraham Lincoln, Adolf Hitler, Barack Obama and Pope Francis are just some that are very much linked to the word "leadership". In fact, these names may even be synonymous to it. And it isn't surprising because one of the ways people become leaders is through their personal traits.

In the early days of management study, it was believed that people like the ones I mentioned possess traits or qualities that separate them from what I'd call "mere mortals" or ordinary people and made them into the leaders that they are. Further, it was initially believed that these characteristics or traits were fixed for life – unchanging and stable. With this point of view, early leadership studies focuses on identifying personal characteristics and traits – including "quantifying" methods – for selecting the best leaders.

The first traits that were identified with being leaders in the earliest studies were dominance, energy, self-confidence, intelligence and task and activity-related knowledge. In succeeding studies, however, that list continued to grow exponentially up to a point where there was way too much leadership-related traits that such a list became impractical already. It's also worth mentioning that the results of said studies tend to be inconsistent.

To be specific, let's look at height as being one of them. While it's true that Abraham Lincoln was a giant of a man at that time (6 feet and 4 inches tall), Napoleon Bonaparte and Adolf Hitler simply demolished that belief, standing at a mere 5 feet 2 inches tall and 5 feet 8 inches, respectively. Other crazier traits that were believed initially to be related to leadership were handwriting, zodiac signs and even body shape. It was because of these and other crazy ideas that the traits leadership approach was abandoned.

But why include this in this e-book? It's because recently, there's renewed interest due to researchers identifying a limited set of traits that have more logical and scientific bases. These include EQ, charisma, drive and motivation.

Chapter 3 – Behavioral Leadership Approach

When experts initially ditched the traits approach to leadership, they shifted their attention to the relationship of observable actions or activities. As such, these experts conducted studies to find out if there are any particular behaviors that can be inextricably linked to leadership. The assumption? Effective leaders' behaviors were significantly different from those that are ineffective. It further assumed that such behaviors are applicable across the board.

Center Of Attention

Significant studies were conducted to determine any behavioral patterns persisted among leaders who have led their groups to perform successfully or effectively. In such studies, 2 sets of behaviors were discovered: employee-centered behaviors and job-centered ones.

Employee-centered leaders are those who believe that a team's efficiency or effectiveness is dependent on how well the team members' human needs were addressed. On the other hand, job-centered leaders believe that such efficiency or effectiveness rested primarily on the job itself, e.g., procedures, cascading of instructions, etc. The studies showed that only one of these approaches could be implemented because they are complete opposites of each other and that employee-centered behavior has significantly higher chances of making a group perform effectively.

Relationships

Other studies were conducted through questionnaires given to subordinates wherein they were asked to assess their leaders' behaviors. Researchers were able to determine several behavioral patterns but they felt only 2 were significant enough to study further: consideration and initiating-structure.

As the name implies, consideration is where leaders consider their subordinates' ideas and feelings, even respecting them. In this behavior, the leader-subordinate relationship is a 2-way one of mutual respect and trust.

Under the initiating-structure, the leader informs his or her subordinates of their roles as well as the expectations of them. The leader also creates a way for him or her to communicate with subordinates and vice-versa and the means for the team to achieve its objectives.

The Grid

Another approach to leadership behavior is known as the Leadership Grid or, The Grid. Originally referred to as the managerial grid, it is a system of analyzing different styles of leadership and based on that, train managers towards a particular leadership style that's believed to be the optimal one for the team.

Under The Grid, there are 5 major styles of leadership:

- Country Club: This leadership style puts a premium on team members' needs for satisfying work relationships. This usually leads to a working atmosphere and tempo that's friendly and comfortable.

- Middle-Of-The-Road: As the name implies, this style is all about balancing team members' morale and team production.

- Impoverished: This leadership style wants to reduce effort exertion to a minimum that's enough for enabling the team to get the work done.

- Authority-Compliance: This leadership style focuses more on team production, looking at team members merely as means to achieve them and their concerns as "hindrances" to productivity.

- Team Management: This leadership style's main goal is to maximize team productivity by maximizing its team member's relationships and morale.

Although the behavioral approach is much different from the traits approach, one thing that ties them together is the tendency to make generic prescriptions as to what makes for effective leaders.

Alan Anderson

Chapter 4 – Situational Leadership Approach

Under this approach, experts believe that a leader should be able to behave differently according to the peculiar needs of different situations. With this approach, the goal is to identify situational factors and the way each of them relate with one another in order to find out what particular leadership behavior is appropriate. Before looking at the different models under this approach, let's take a look the foundational approach for these.

Continuum Of Leadership Behavior

Robert Tannenbaum and Warren Schmidt conceptualized the continuum, integrating some behaviors that leaders may want to consider in specific situations. On one end of this continuum is the leader having the sole discretion or prerogative to make decisions for the team and on the other end is subordinates being able to decide freely without need for the leader's guidance. The balance or proportion of the leader's authority and the subordinates' freedom depends on the different qualities of a team's situation, manager and team members.

Managers' qualities to be considered include his or her feelings of security, trust and confidence in the subordinates, personal biases and values, among other things. Qualities to be considered for subordinates include the capacity for tolerating ambiguity, willingness to take on responsibilities, interest in expectations and problems, and their need for independence. Situational factors for consideration include the team's effectiveness, organizational structure and time pressure, among several other factors.

Situation Leadership Models

<u>LPC Leadership Theory</u>

Fred Fiedler developed this theory. This attempts to reconcile and explain a team's situational complexities and its leader's personality and was originally called the contingency leadership theory. Only because of the original name's generic meaning was it changed into its more renowned name: Least-Preferred-Coworker or LPC.

Under this leadership model, it is proposed that a leader's effectiveness is contingent on his or her team's situation. However, the theory doesn't just end there – it also attempts to find out why particular discrepancies happen and how to best combine certain leader types and situations for effective team performance.

Under LPC, Fiedler asked leaders to identify the last person they would want to work with again – their least preferred coworker – and rate that person on a scale of positive factors such as cheerfulness, helpfulness and friendliness, among others on one end and on the other end, negative factors like gloominess, unhelpfulness and unfriendliness, among others. When a leader gives a low score for that person, he or she's considered to be a low LPC kind of leader. A low LPC score leader tends to put more importance on productivity versus relationships and will only tend to the latter when work is performed according to expectations. A high score for that least preferred co-worker makes him or her a high LPC leader. A high LPC score leader tends to have positively close working relationships with his or her subordinates – even supportive to the point of putting more importance to the relationship over productivity.

Fiedler came up with words to describe a leader's personality traits-leadership relationship: Task Motivation and Relationship Motivation. Task motivation is akin to the job-centered and initiating structure leader behaviors. Relationship motivation is similar to the behavioral approach of employee-centeredness and consideration leadership behavior. How are these different from the behavioral approach models? These are based on leaders' personalities, which tend to be generally the same for any particular leader.

In terms of the different situations leaders lead their teams in, there are 3 factors that determine just how favorable situations are to a leader in order of importance (most to least):

- Relationships: Referring to the relationship between the leader and members, this refers to the level of confidence, trust and respect in and for each other. High levels indicate good relationships, which are favorable for the leader – and vice versa.

- Structure: This refers to tasks' level of simplicity, understandability, clarity and how routine they are. The assumption under LPC is that tasks that are more structured require less supervision and minimal monitoring are more favorable for leaders than those that are otherwise because it allows him or her to focus on more important activities of the team.

- Power: This is about how much power or authority the leader has that comes with the leadership position. It's more favorable for a leader if he or she has higher position power, i.e., power to promote or punish subordinate, reward them or assign their tasks.

The studies conducted by Fiedler on the interaction between group performance, situational favorableness and leader motivation resulted in the identification of 3 possible situations: favorable, moderately favorable and unfavorable. Leadership styles were also recommended for each particular situation.

If the leader's relationship with his or her subordinates is good and the tasks or jobs are structured, his or her situation may be considered as favorable. In this kind of situation, Fiedler recommends a task-oriented behavior or leadership style.

If the leader's relationship with his or her members as well as the structuredness of the tasks or jobs is just so-so, i.e., middle of the road kind of thing neither here nor there, the situation may be considered moderately favorable. Under this situation, a person-oriented behavior or leadership style is recommended.

If the leader's relationship with his or her subordinates isn't anywhere near good and the tasks or job are loosely defined, i.e., unstructured, the situation is considered unfavorable for the leader. As such, a task-oriented behavior or leadership style is recommended.

Although this model is plausible, it isn't perfect and has its own share of concerns. For one, what if the leader's personality isn't quite up to par or doesn't match with his or her situation…what then? To be more specific, what if the leader is person-oriented but his or her situation is considered unfavorable? The implication of this is that if the basis for leadership behavior is personality trait, then a leader who finds him or herself in a mismatched situation won't be able to adapt well enough to be effective. Under this assumption, the team needs to adjust to the leader, i.e., re-engineer jobs and team structure to make it compatible with the leader.

Another concern is validity. The model is quite controversial because of conflicting results of studies reported. Some of the models flaws according to experts are unrealistic assumptions on leaders' inflexibility and insufficient research. If that's the case, why the heck are we even looking at this model, eh? I knew you'd ask that!

We do so because the model, for its flaws and shortcomings, isn't totally worthless. In fact, it contributed significantly to the evolution of the study of leadership because it brought the focus back on leadership situations that take into great consideration the team's or organization's situational effects on leadership effectiveness.

Path-Goal Model

Similar to the LPC model, this model also focuses on situational leadership behavior instead of their personality traits. The difference being, however, is that the Path-Goal Model – PGM for brevity – believes leaders can adjust their styles depending on their situations. PGM's foundation is one of Psychology's major theories – the Expectancy Theory or ET (no alien conspiracy theorists, please) for short.

ET suggests that any person's behaviors and attitudes are dependent on their expectations about the outcomes of their tasks as well as how much those outcomes mean to them. Based on this, PGM establishes the case that leaders can motivate their team members by behaving in ways that influence the latter's expectations. To simply it, leaders can motivate their subordinates into performing well by clearly communicating to them how they can achieve their desired outcomes or rewards. As such, it also suggests, albeit indirectly, that leaders' behaviors aren't fixed, as the LPC model suggests.

PGM enumerates 4 different kinds of leaders' behavior:

- Directive: Here, the leader's subordinates know exactly what the leaders wants from them, how to be able to achieve them, when these are expected to be accomplished and by which standards will their performances be evaluated.

- Supportive: Leaders show concern about his or her subordinates' personal needs, status and well being as well as being friendly towards them.

- Participative: Here, leaders ask for their team members' take on team issues as well as their suggestions and feedback prior to deciding on a course of action.

- Achievement-Oriented: Under this behavior, leaders give their subordinates challenging goals to achieve, expects them to perform well and expresses his or her confidence in their abilities to do so.

Unlike in LPC where leaders are limited to set behaviors, PGM believes leaders can customize their leadership styles depending on their teams' particular situations.

PGM present to factors that can influence the extent of leaders' behaviors ability to make their subordinates feel satisfied:

- Personal Characteristics Of Subordinates: There are 2 key personal characteristics involved here: Locus of control and the subordinates' perception of their abilities.

Locus of control pertains to the subordinate's view or belief on how much of what happens to them can they control. The more a subordinate believes that he or she is primarily responsible for or has control over what happens to them, the more they are open or function better under a participative style of leadership. Consequently, the less control a subordinate feels he or she has over what happens to them, they'll be less open to and perform less in a participative leadership style. They'll be more open to and function better under a directive leadership style because they know that they have less responsibility over their performance and as such, there isn't much consequence to them.

A subordinate's perception of his or her ability to perform a task is another personal characteristic of subordinates' that determine the leadership style they'll most probably be able to thrive in. Subordinates who believe they are very much up to the task may thrive more under a participative or an achievement oriented leadership style because they are confident they can do their jobs well. On the other hand, subordinates who have doubts if they can do their jobs well may thrive better under a directive style of leadership.

- Environment: According to PGM, there are 3 characteristics of a team's environment that can help determine the most appropriate leadership style: task structure, formal authority and primary work group. PGM proposes that the most appropriate leadership behavior or style is one that can help his or her subordinates deal with the uncertainties that any or all of the 3 environmental characteristics may bring.

Vroom's Tree

This model, which features the use of a decision tree, was created by among other people, a person whose last name is – surprise – Vroom! He actually had help from Philip Yetton and Arthur Jago but primarily, this was his work. This model assumes that situational factors affect the extent of subordinates' participation in decision-making activities. In other words, there's no single best process for making team decisions for all situations.

PGM suggests that leaders utilize either of 2 decision trees that begin with the leader assessing his or her team's situation according to multiple factors that can affect decision-making. This assessment helps the manager navigate the decision tree's paths toward an ideal course of action. The reason for using 2 decision trees is that one is for when the leader has the luxury of time and would like to take the opportunity to develop his or her subordinates' decision-making skills while the other is when the leader needs to make a decision ASAP.

In making use of Vroom's decision tree, there are 5 leadership decision styles to choose from:

- Deciding, where the leader alone decides for the team;

- Delegating, where the leader let's the team identify the problems, create the necessary parameters for solving them and formulate solutions to address said problems;

- Individual Consultations, where the leader talks to each and every member of his or her group before making his or her decision;

- Group Consultations, where the leader collectively meets with his or her subordinates to get their opinions and views before deciding on a course of action; and

- Facilitating, where the leader merely facilitates the team's collective discussion on how to solve a problem after he or she first identifies and presents the problem to be solved to the team and creating the parameters in which to solve it.

Because this process can be quite complex to facilitate, Vroom created software that helps leaders accurately and quickly evaluate their teams' situations and identify appropriate courses of action according to the level of their subordinates' participation in the process. Some of the leading companies who are using different versions of this software include Litton Industries, Halliburton Company and Borland International.

Leader-Member Exchange Model

This model, created by Fred Dansereau and George Graen, highlights the importance of leaders' relationships with each and every one of his or her subordinates or followers and each of these relationships is referred to as a vertical dyad. Particularly, this model is somewhat different from the early situational leadership models in that individual relationships are considered instead of with the whole team. The primary way of evaluating each relationship is whether or not the particular subordinate is within or outside the leaders inner circle.

When the subordinate is inside the leader's inner circle or in-group, that person tends to get higher-ranking or level tasks and consequently, more privileges and opportunities compared to those who are outside of it. Subordinates who are outside the leader's inner circle are noticed less by the leader and as such, tend to get assigned to less meaningful tasks with less opportunities and privileges. This suggests that subjectivity is a key consideration.

Hershey And Blanchard Model

Referred to HBM for brevity, this model submits that leadership style or behavior should adjust to the readiness levels of subordinates, i.e., their levels of willingness to take on responsibility, experience, competence and motivation. To get a better understanding of this, let's take a look at a situation.

If subordinates aren't ready for the tasks at hand, the leader should primarily use a directive leadership style, i.e., clearly define the subordinates' roles and give them specific directions for the assigned tasks. Over time as the subordinates become more competent, experienced, motivated and willing to take responsibility, the leader can then cut back on the directive style and move towards a delegating style instead.

Alan Anderson

Chapter 5 – Subordinates' Perspective Models

Another way of looking at leadership style is through the eyes of those being led – the subordinates or the followers. This model or approach to leadership highlights the importance of how subordinates or team members look at or feel about their leaders in terms of effective team performance. There are 3 leadership styles or models that are based on subordinates' perceptions of their leaders:

- Transformational Leadership: Under this model, a distinction is made between leading for stability and leading for change. From this vantage point, a leader needs to start and manage occasional major changes within the team like redefining team culture and mergers with other teams. This kind of leadership pertains to a collection of leadership abilities that allow the leader to identify, guide and execute necessary changes in the team.

- Charismatic Leadership: This kind of leadership is founded on a leader's attractiveness to his or her subordinates or followers, which inspire the latter to support, accept and follow his or her decisions and actions. The belief is that given all things equal among different leaders, the one who is most charismatic – has the most attractive traits and qualities – will be able to command more respect, support and willingness from subordinates en route to effective team performance. You may be very familiar with this leadership style. Steve Jobs, Oprah Winfrey, Sir Richard Branson and Barack Obama are some of the world's most recognizable leaders who are very charismatic.

Charismatic leadership has 3 important ingredients: envisioning, energizing and enabling. Envisioning refers to a leader's ability to identify future patterns and trends, set the bar high in terms of performance and cast the vision to his or her subordinates via modeling behavior. Energizing refers to influence and inspire his or her subordinates towards achieving team goals and objectives by personally showing confidence, records of success and excitement. Enabling is about giving subordinates the necessary support – emotional and resource-wise – to help them achieve what's expected of them and consequently, make the team perform effectively.

- Attributions Of Leadership: It's human nature for people to link observed behavior to some meaning or cause. It's from this perspective that we understand the attribution of leadership point of view that subordinates tend to evaluate their leaders' powers and abilities based on the latter's observed leadership behaviors.

A good way to illustrate this perspective is through a group of people trapped in an elevator. The first person to take charge of the situation confidently will be followed by the other trapped passengers or will help them feel things will turn out well. If on the other hand, the same person showed lack of confidence or conviction in taking charge, the other trapped passengers will swiftly realize he's not a leader and as such, they'll either panic, won't follow him or both.

It's worth noting that the best situation to observe a leader's behavior is during a crisis. It's where the real personality shows up. Later in the book, you'll learn how to handle crises effectively.

Chapter 6 – Leadership Alternatives And Neutralizers

Believe it or not, there will be times when exercising leadership can be inappropriate. Yes, despite the importance of such as promoted by practically all organizational experts worth their salt, leadership may be unnecessary or even irrelevant in quite a few situations. What determines this is collectively called leadership substitutes or alternatives.

Leadership alternatives pertain to things that override a leader's ability to influence or control his or her subordinates' performance and job satisfaction. Simply put, these are things that enable subordinates to function well and perform effectively even without the participation of their leaders.

On the other hand, there are also things that render a leader's attempts to lead his or her team. These things are referred to as leadership neutralizers.

Factors

One of the things that can either is an alternative to leadership or a neutralizer is a person's characteristics. These include his or her experience, professionalism, indifference to rewards, motivation and training. A good way to look at this would be to consider a policeman.

If and when a crime is being committed in a neighborhood, a cop doesn't need to get his chief's go signal or authorization to neutralize or apprehend the criminal elements. He or she can respond immediately and act accordingly because of his or her formal authority, training, experience and expertise in handling such situations, and issued equipment.

In a similar light, if that cop's superior is so inexperienced as to order him or her to do something risky and foolish, that cop can override or neutralize that superior's authority and act accordingly to prevent further escalation of the criminal situation.

For something to effectively substitute or neutralize leadership, it should be highly structured, automated, highly controlled, highly satisfying and has a built-in mechanism for feedback. Examples of these include a team's cohesiveness and culture. For organizations as a whole, substitutes and neutralizers include strict procedures, rigid rules, clear objectives and goals, and a comprehensive rewards system.

Chapter 7 – Management

Now that you have a good picture of what leadership is and the ways to exercise leadership in general, we'll now focus on your being an effective manager. As a manager, you are key to your organization's success. Hence, it's important that you are an effectively good one.

One of the things you'll need to be as a manager is be a technically adept one. In particular, you should know your team very well, from its functions to how it's supposed to operate to the best available practices. If you're a sales manager, for example, you need to be a good salesman first and foremost. The same goes for being a branch manager of a bank. You'll need to be very adept not just with banking procedures and practices but also most especially with banking laws. Otherwise, you won't just be effective – you can also get into legal trouble.

Another thing you'll need to be able to do as a manager is to handle your team's activities very well. As such, you'll need to be comfortable with handling changes, be able to continuously improve the way your team does its things, handle crises superbly, focus on your team's clients, efficiently conduct meetings, plan well and organize excellently.

But more than just managing and developing your team well, you need to be able to manage and develop yourself well too. Part of this means you'll have to learn how to achieve good results, assert yourself well, communicate clearly, think well, make decisions quickly and confidently, manage your schedule well and take time to continuously build up your skills.

Lastly, you need to be a good leader. As mentioned earlier, being a leader and manager aren't exclusive – they're intertwined and you can't be good at one without the other. Managing requires leading people – that's why you need to be a good one.

Your Role As Manager

As a manager, you'll play a very important role, especially in terms of giving your team procedural and professional guidance. For your team to be considered effective, it must be able to achieve the goals for which it was formed or created. It must be able to maximize its resources too.

A key ingredient in effective teams is synergy, which is the ability to get more results than simply the sum of each resource's results. In short, 1+1 isn't just 2. With synergy, 1+1=3. Synergy distinguishes good teams from average ones.

To make your team effective and manage it well, you as a manager need to maximize your team's inherent strengths and advantages. These strengths and advantages include:

- Each Team Member's Knowledge And Skills: When added together, there's synergy in your team members' individual skills and knowledge. As such, you must be able to know each of your team members or subordinates very well on a personal level. If your team's too big that it's impractical to do so, you should at least be able to know very well the people who you identify to be key members of your team, around whom the rest of your subordinates or members can rally.

Without a close enough relationship with your subordinates, or at least with the key ones, you won't be in a position to maximize their individual strengths and minimize the impact of their individual weaknesses, which are both key to maximizing your team's performance.

- Harmony In Diversity: Chances are, each of your subordinates or team members have different levels of working and problem solving experience as well as different personalities and strengths. Instead of being a reason for discord and tension, why not make it your team's strength?

In order for you to do that, you'll need to be open-minded, humble and secure with yourself. When you're like that, you can effectively foster an atmosphere of harmony in the midst of divergent interests, opinions and levels of skill and experience. If you're close-minded, proud and insecure on the other hand, you won't be able to encourage your subordinates to express themselves – particularly their strengths and potentially productive ideas – and prevent your team from potentially achieving groundbreaking levels of success or avoiding potential team-breaking failures.

- Commitment And Acceptance: Two of the most important aspects of effective team performance are subordinates' commitment and acceptance of the team as a whole and of each other individually. As the saying goes, united teams stand, divided they fall.

To be an effective manager of an effective team, you'll need to foster good working – and if possible, personal – relationships between you and your subordinates and among themselves. While it may be impossible to make each and every one of them their very own best friends, it is highly possible that you can create an environment that is conducive for subordinates's acceptance of and commitment to each other individually and to the team as a whole.

The Bible says that 3 strands of cord can't easily be torn and as a team, the extent to which you can bind your subordinates together like a "3 strands of cords" is the extent that you can create one solid and effective team.

- Progress: Another way you can encourage and inspire your subordinates for effective team performance is to give them the opportunities – if they desire so – to take on gradually increasing work responsibilities and challenges to help them not just "shine" but also build up their skills, talents and confidence. When your subordinates continue to improve and excel as a result of such improvements, you will enjoy the benefit of managing a progressively improving team.

If you don't provide such opportunities and if you don't empower and enable your subordinates to take advantage of such opportunities, their skills and minds will stagnate, they'll probably grow bored and become unmotivated and eventually become less productive. At the end of the day, it'll rebound back to your team's overall performance. That's why it's important to empower them and give them opportunities to build up their skills and confidence.

- Disputes: This is one of those double-edged sword kinds of things. If you handle them well, they can be a great source of growth and improvement for the team. If you don't, then it can cut real deep and hurt your team's performance.

Don't' be afraid of disputes – but don't go chasing them and deliberately creating situations for such either. Simply embrace them when it happens and handle them accordingly. You'll learn how to manage these well in Chapter XX.

Managing Effective Teams: What To Avoid

Equally important when it comes to managing effective teams are the things you'll need to avoid or prevent. The following are things that can minimize or even overpower whatever strengths your team may inherently possess:

Management: Take Charge of Your Team

- Peer Pressure: As the manager and the leader, you are to be the ultimate authority in your team. As such, you need to be able to assert yourself with minimal dissention from your subordinates. You can't afford to be pressured by anyone else – either other managers who have no business handling your team or your own subordinates.

If you fail to hold your own and allow yourself to be pressured into making acting and deciding on your team's concerns, you increase your risk of not being able to effectively lead your team. It's because if this happens often, your subordinates' respect for you as a leader may significantly erode to the point they no longer trust and follow you with the belief that you're incompetent.

So learn the art of being both assertively firm and encouraging. It'll help you go a long way as an effective manager of an effective team.

- Dominance By Any Subordinate: Aside from not letting the team dominate you (peer pressure), you should also make sure that no other team member dominates the team. When you have a dominant subordinate, you run the risk of losing control of your team to that person and either your team becomes ineffective due to insubordination or that dominant subordinate gets promoted to your position. Those should be enough incentives to prevent this from happening, eh?

There's a right way of doing this, though – and it's not through sheer power play and dominance. Here's where being a leader comes into play. You'll need to be influential, assertive and encouraging in order to keep any of your subordinates from being tempted or encourage dominating the team.

- Politics: If politics (in the traditional sense, that is) is bad for the country, how much more is it for your own team?

> As a manager, you must do your best to minimize politics in your team.

One of the reasons for this is that political compromises tend to harm your team's effectiveness and goals because compromises, by nature, require giving up some important things to accommodate the other party. For example, if rumormongering is rampant in your team, those who are subject of such harsh rumors may be forced to either leave the team or sabotage his or her work as a means of getting back. The ultimate loser in this case is the team as a whole.

The best way to minimize this is by fostering a good working atmosphere among the team members or subordinates. Politicking or gossiping happens only among people who have poor relationships. When relationships are deep, there's less room or incentive for politicking or gossiping about each other.

A good way to minimize this too is by being clear from the get go that politicking and gossiping is frowned upon in your team and that doing so has its consequences.

- Distractions: Picture, if you will, a target-shooting booth at your local carnival. Have you ever experienced shooting at a target and for some reason, your shot's just off the mark? You may have tried spotting targets smack dead at the center of carnival rifles' sights but still manage to shoot about an inch or two away from the target? It's probably because the barrels of such rifles are ever so slightly bent – off by just a degree or two. Even if the bend is just one or two degrees off-center, it has a great impact in your shooting accuracy that it can throw off your shot by several inches.

Distractions are like bent or misaligned barrels of rifles...even just a little can throw your team off track from achieving its goals. And just like raffle barrels that are off by just one or two degrees, they can be very subtle that they don't seem to be distractions at all. That's why minimizing – eliminating if possible – distractions is both important and not easy at all. Often times, distractions take the disguise of being "related" and "relevant" to your team's goals while in reality, they're anything but.

- Groupthink: If it's your first time to encounter this word, it refers to a team's tendency do make decisions – particularly important ones – based on consensus or voting. This kind of decision-making process is in and by itself neither wise nor unwise. However, using this as the primary way of deciding on your team's important courses of action is what makes it unwise.

Your risk of succumbing to this practice is much higher if you're the type of leader who puts team harmony on a pedestal or if you're the type who avoids taking responsibility for your team's actions and results. This is one of the most serious errors you can ever commit as a manager and as such, you should exert all possible efforts to avoid committing this mistake.

One of the best ways to minimize this is to first develop your strong leadership qualities such as taking on responsibilities, confidence, self-assertion and decisiveness. It will also help if you can diversify the membership of your team, i.e., people of different backgrounds and expertise.

The extent to which you're able to maximize your team's strengths and advantages as well as minimizing or avoiding altogether the afore-mentioned practices is the extent to which you maximize your team's performance en route to being an effective one. As such, this seems to be more of an art than science. It'll take practice to be able to get a good feel on how to do it well.

General Strategies For Managing A Winning Team

You, as a manager, are only as effective as your team is. This means you should put a premium in developing a strong and efficient team and to be able to do so, you'll need to do your homework, i.e., plan and learn well.

The following are some of the general strategies you can learn well and incorporate in your plan to make your team a winning one:

- **Identify:** Your team's effectiveness depends a lot on maximizing your team members' individual strengths, right? But how can you maximize something you don't know exists. Hence, identifying their strengths is the crucial first strategy for managing a winning team.

Some of the things you need to consider when trying to identify these things are the team's tenure (permanent or temporary), the nature of the jobs performed, your team's structure and place in the whole organization, how long has it been in existence and the degree of ease or difficulty in finding people to take the place or substitute for existing team members.

When managers form a new but temporary team, they're usually concerned with the interpersonal as well as technical skills of the people they're considering to recruit. Of particular concern as such people's skills in relation to the team's function, how to distribute authority or power among selected members of the team and if these selected members can adequately represent their constituents.

As a manager, you should seriously consider balancing the team's available resources and your team's identified strengths – and even weaknesses – if you are to manage a winning team, regardless of tenure. This is where an earlier emphasis on knowing your team members well comes into play. The more you know them, the better you'll be able to strike the optimal balance between your team's strengths and available resources.

- Incorporate: After identifying your team's key strengths, it's time to incorporate these into your team's profile. What this means is you need to wisely use these strengths or characteristics and maximize them by, among other ways, linking them together. To this extent, you'll need to be able to find out just much of these characteristics or strengths are exhibited in your team. You can do this through the paper and pencil questionnaire method, observing your team directly or conducting interviews.

One concern with this method is that it may take time for your team members to honestly answer them because doing so puts them at risk of having to be vulnerable. The only way they'll allow themselves to be vulnerable is when they trust the person conducting the survey – you! For this to be successfully carried out, you need to have a good enough relationship with your subordinates.

Another concern with this method is clarification. There will be times that participants in this survey may not understand the question and as such, may not be able to answer it correctly, if at all. The remedy for this is for you to be present as they answer the survey questionnaires.

Another way of getting such information is by directly observing your team members at work. This is, however, time consuming. It's because as a manager, you'll need to allot significant blocks of time to simply watch and observe your subordinates or team members, recording and evaluating your observations. There really isn't any other way...unless you install a hidden camera and audio recorder and run through it on your spare time.

Oh, and speaking of time consuming, you can't just observe them one time. It's because people in general have a tendency to put their best foot forward when they know they're being observed and as such, you'll have to "wear them out" by observing them longer. As mentioned earlier, a good way to shortcut the process is by installing a hidden camera and audio recorder so that they'll act naturally. However, you risk losing their trust and confidence if they find out.

With the direct observation method, you already have an idea of what particular skills or behavior to look for. Otherwise, it'll even be more time consuming than it already is and render the whole activity more impractical than practical.

Another strategy is interviewing your team members, which can be viewed as a possible compromise between the first to strategies I've identified. Through interviews, you can interact directly with your team members, observe their non-verbal cues (body language speaks louder than verbal) and ask follow-up questions real time. As such, it'll be very beneficial to you if you learn the art of reading body language.

You can also use your interviews with team members to supplement whatever data or information you may have gathered through questionnaires and observations. When well designed, consistent and structured, interviews can be really effective in helping you get the information you need.

One commonality this has with questionnaires is that you'll need to have a good enough relationship with your team members in order to be able to draw out honest answers. If you don't strike them as someone who can be trusted, don't expect to draw out accurate answers. You might as well not utilize this strategy if that's the case.

Chapter 8 – Learning About Your Team

When faced with people that you don't know, how can you know who is capable of doing what? What is a good idea is to give your team members a task at the beginning of a project. Get them to write down what they feel are their strengths and weaknesses. Everyone will write a good list of strengths, but asked to face up to weaknesses team members may have to reflect a little. Let them reflect and give these to you on your second meeting.

Getting to know your team's strengths and weaknesses

The first meeting should discuss what the project is, the time scale you have to get the job done in and give people time to voice their ideas. From this meeting, you should see who the bright sparks are. You will also find out who are the ones who are more likely to follow than to lead. Using the same kind of format of getting to know your team as Richard Branson uses, you need to decide who does what fairly quickly, but you also need to base this on your knowledge of the team member's strengths and weaknesses. Ask members of the team to hand in their lists so that you can take a look at what they have to say. I always ask them to list the following:

- Personal Strengths
- Personal Weaknesses
- Where they feel they fit into the team
- Level of expertise and specialty

Remember this is how the worker sees their role but what they see may not be the same as the boss sees their role. People are quick to extol their virtues, but you need to know what their levels of expertise are in certain fields. For example, on one project, we had to do a lot of number crunching and of course someone with accountancy experience was more valuable to that task than someone with no accounting experience. Thus, you fit the members of your team to the particular tasks that you have in mind and make sure that all of those tasks put together can come up with the required result within the given time.

I said right at the beginning that there is no such thing as a bad team member. There may be members who are less capable than others, but they all have their role to play. Among the jobs that go to make up any given project, there will be tedious jobs that the bright sparks don't want to do, but that those with less expectations are actually quite happy to perform.

Dealing with deadlines and check points

Split the job into a series of checkpoints, so that meetings are kept to a minimum, but so that each member of the team knows what the deadline is for each step of the way and work toward that deadline. When the meetings are held, you have a better idea of the progress and can adjust your staff if you find the project is running behind.

It is valuable to know your team. Having their work experience, you can decide who should be trusted with which part of the task and also who can work with whom. The problem comes when you have personality conflicts and this is dealt with in a separate chapter. If you find that particular members like to work on their own, that's also valuable information as placing them with others may even slow them down.

One thing to be aware of is that the descriptions that your team members give you will give you a better idea of who they are. Remember that blowing one's own trumpet doesn't necessarily mean that the member who does it is as valuable as he sees himself to be. I learned that with one team that I had who had given me very compelling reasons to trust him with a large part of the project, and I am glad that I set deadlines throughout the job because had it not been for this, I might not have known until the end that he wasn't actually capable of what he told me he was capable of. If this happens to you, your deadlines will be able to help you make adjustments so that you don't make an absolute idiot of yourself when the end of the project nears.

You will also get to know which members of the team need more guidance than others. There are always those who need approval and will seek out your attention and these should perhaps be placed with those who like doling out approval and encouragement as this can save you a lot of time.

Your team members need to do the job that you have been entrusted to do. As a team leader, you need to get to know them, to trust them and somehow make sure that they trust you. Let them know at all times that you are approachable and if things are not hitting target dates, you need to know as soon as possible so that adjustments can be made to get your project back on track.

Alan Anderson

Chapter 9 – Grooming Team Members and Developing Skills

It's not enough that you know your team's strengths and weaknesses, both as a whole and individually. You need to build your team members up in terms of skills and responsibilities if you want your team to be a winningly effective one. Like athletes, the day your team's skills and abilities plateau is the day it starts to stagnate and eventually, go down the road to ineffectiveness.

Of particular interest are your team's weaknesses first. Why? Because apart from being an area for productivity improvement, weaknesses can also pose risks to whatever strengths your team already has. Think of it as both strengthening and protecting your team.

The following are strategies that you can employ in order to both strengthen and protect your winningly effective team.

Identify The Weakest Links

Secretly, split your team into 2 groups using either a pen and paper or a spreadsheet on your computer: those that are highly capable and those whose performance leaves something to be desired. This gives you the benefit of knowing who and what to focus your team building activities and resources on first. Again, the weakest links tend to pose the highest performance risk for the team and it only makes sense to prioritize them first over those that have lower or minimal risk.

Your team's poor performance can be due to gaps between your team members' skills and experience, job requirements and available resources. The smaller such gaps are, the higher are your team's chances of performing effectively. Because you're the manager, it's your responsibility to identify the weakest links in order to strengthen them.

It's neither a crime nor a sin to ask for help if you believe you're not equipped to do this well. That's why there are consultants, both internal and external, that you can tap in order to get this thing done right. For one, you can tap your human resources department's (assumed) expertise in identifying the weakest links.

Deciding Optimally For Weak Links

As today's business have grown more unique and complex, simply going for a shotgun-approach to dealing with weak links isn't wise. It's like giving the whole basketball team uniforms of the same size. Some of them will be hip-hoppishly big while some will be as tight as halter-tops. Bottom line: which weak link should be prioritized and what sequence should be followed in doing so? As a manager, you'll need to come up with a number of criteria for deciding how to best proceed in terms of addressing your weakest links.

Part of making such decisions is being able to objectively identify your team's limitations in order to work around them and make the team more effective. Take for example a team that is responsible for producing 1,000 pairs of sneakers daily that is able to produce only 900 pairs. Further, let's say that the whole production line consists of 3 phases:

- Phase 1: Cutting and preparation of materials, done by 11 people who can prepare at most materials good for 1,200 pairs of said sneakers.

- Phase 2: Assembling of the sneakers, done by 10 people who can assemble at most 900 pairs daily.

- Phase 3: Packaging of the sneakers done by 5 people who can pack 950 pairs daily at most.

Looking at the 3 phases, it becomes obvious that the problems are phases 2 and 3 – they're the weaknesses. If you have limited time and resources, which of the two should you address first? If you address phase 3 first and get them up to par with the 1,000 pairs daily requirement, will the team be able to maximize resources? No, because if the phase 3 people increase their capacity to 1,000, it won't mean much if they only receive 900 pairs daily. You'll still just end up with excess capacity of 100 pairs daily. If you address phase 2 first, you'll be able to maximize existing resources.

The ideal solution of course is to address both phases simultaneously. But for examples' sake, we placed a limitation because in most cases, your team's resources will be limited and you'll need to make wise decisions as to what weak link to prioritize first as well as the sequencing.

Choose The Optimal Strategy

Based on what you've identified to be the priority areas and sequence of events, you can now decide on what particular strategy to apply to strengthen your team's weak areas. Is it to hire more people? Do you simply need to retrain them? Or do you need to replace them either with new and more efficient people or with machines?

Your choice of strategy will be dependent on available resources, both financial and manpower. In a perfect world, you can always go for the optimal strategy. However, such a world doesn't exist and chances are, you'll have to work around budgetary and manpower constraints.

Alan Anderson

Chapter 10 – Your Coaching Skills

If you have been made a team leader, it's because your company has recognized something in you that gives them the opinion that you can lead a team. That doesn't mean getting the team to do all of the work and sitting on your laurels while they do. In most cases, you will be expected to direct members of your team and to help them to grasp what it is that they are expected to do.

Improving your coaching skills

A good team leader is one that realizes that coaching plays a part in what they do. CEOs who are good at leading teams give their team members a lot of encouragement and listen to ideas as well as teaching their team members skills that give those team members more confidence. There is a certain amount of trust that you need to be able to give key members, but remember that the more you motivate your team members to perform, the less you have to actually chase them up near the end of the project because of disappointing results.

Richard Branson said that he was always particular in his choice of leaders because these were people who shared his vision and who were able to pass on that same enthusiasm to others. His empire grew because of this trust placed in his leadership members and in your case, you need to gather ideas – to help people to understand different concepts and to coach them so that they perform and are pleased to perform with the same amount of enthusiasm all the way through the project.

Your coaching skills will be put to the test. You may have to collate reports, liaise with team members and get them into an enthusiastic way of thinking especially if things are falling behind. Don't ever ridicule a member of your team or admonish a team member for failures. This is always something that demoralizes a team member and you may as well cut someone from your already shorthanded team if that's the attitude that you take. Being calm, even when things are not going to plan, you set them the perfect example and that's what team management is all about. Get them to look up to you, not to dread encounters with you. Get them to share your vision and to want to succeed.

One CEO I worked with was a great character. We all loved this guy because he actually made us want to succeed and gave us all the right messages. I remember coming out of his office one day wondering about why he enthused me so much, even though we knew that a lot of what he was giving us was sales talk. The fact was that as a leader, he actually believed what he was telling us and even though he was sometimes wrong, we couldn't fault his enthusiasm and belief in us, as his team. He wasn't the best team leader I had ever known, but he was certainly the most memorable and it may be worthwhile taking a leaf out of his book and remembering to always put a positive spin on everything. People are much more likely to be compliant with your deadlines if you can learn to be diplomatic and helpful, encouraging and friendly but also make sure that your enthusiasm for the job always exceeds that of your team, so that they follow your lead.

The guy that I mentioned above had boundless energy. He had thousands of ideas and some of them were really bad ideas, but as a team leader that knew exactly what he was doing, he knew when to drop ideas that had received a dim reception. Instead of pushing his team to do things he knew that they didn't actually believe in, he learned that part of his job as a team leader was to listen to his team members and recognize it when they came up with better ideas than he did. It worked and invariably the team did come up with better ideas.

Remember to give credit where it is due. One unpopular team leader that I worked under actually took credit for the ideas of his team and that's not very motivating. By giving your team members credit, you actually win more respect from your team and get better results. If a team member comes up with an idea that's better than yours, don't shut it out because you are the leader. Listen to it, appraise it and if there is a reason that it can't be implemented, discuss it. There's nothing more demotivating than thinking that your ideas are never considered or that you are not being given a fair hearing.

If you don't know the answer to a question, use the standard "That's a very good question" ploy to give you time to think of an answer. It always works and it's better for your team to see that you recognize the question as being a very viable one, rather than listen to you stutter your way through trying to answer something without a clue what you are going to say. Learn to change subjects as well, as you may need to use this ploy in times when questions are asked that are irrelevant or of little use to your team or to you.

"I think we have enough to work on from this meeting …" is perhaps a last resort, but it recognizes that your team members really do have their work cut out for them, and it may get you out of having to answer idiot questions thrown in at the end of a meeting.

Alan Anderson

Chapter 11 – Communication

Communication is one of the most vital tools that you have in your workbox as a team leader. You have to enthuse people. Team leaders are the cheerleaders but they are also the people who take the responsibility if the team fails. Thus, you need to practice your communication skills and make sure that you come over as:

- Friendly
- Approachable
- Professional
- Informed

Let's go through those aspects one by one because they are all vital to the experience of being a team leader. Friendliness is what gives you an edge. You can't be on first name terms with people unless you are willing to put yourself out there and let them be on first name terms with you. Whatever gets the job done is the way that you need to move forward. You can't be his or her best friend, but you can be someone who knows that a friendly approach that gives the team equal respect will gain you friendship that will, in turn, give your team the impetus to be loyal.

How entrepreneurs communicate with a team

I looked once at the example that entrepreneurs such as Richard Branson had with his teams. There was an interview on the Internet about this and I remember reading it. He gave his team members sufficient closeness so that they considered him a worthy person within their lives, but he also made himself very approachable at the same time. Some friends that you have in your life are not quite as approachable, but a team leader has to be. He has to put out his ideas and depend upon the team to respond and to respect the eventual decisions that he has to make.

Richard Branson said that he was always careful with his choice of team leaders for a specific purpose. If you cannot trust a team leader to do what it is they need to do, then that makes more work for you in the long run. His recipe for having a company that works so well is to employ team leaders that he trusts and your boss, as a team leader, has placed you in the position of trust. As long as your boss has made it clear what the objective of the team is, it is this that you need to communicate to your team.

Your professionalism will show in your approach. You should be well informed and not give the impression that you need to keep going back to your boss to ask questions because that makes you look ineffective. The whole idea of the team leader thing is that you are in charge of making a certain thing happen and need your team to follow your lead. Leadership of a team means that you need to be aware of your team member's strengths and weaknesses and need to place trust in team members to do what you need them to do.

Learn to communicate your objective clearly

Communication is everything. If you don't communicate effectively, you may give out mixed messages and when deadlines are not met, will wonder why. Be precise in instructions, learn who to lean on for what task and then trust your team members to jump into action, making yourself approachable if they should have a query that they believe may impede their progress.

Management: Take Charge of Your Team

When you first communicate with your team, they will take their lead from the inspiration that you give them. Therefore, if you are not good a speech making or talking without leaving doubt in their minds, you need to brush up on those skills. Confidence is gained when you are able to communicate with authority and answer any questions that team members may pose that affect the project.

In the situation I was faced with, with a hostile team, I managed to get through a very grueling first meeting with the team. They expected me to stumble. They expected to know more than I did about the workings of the company. What they didn't bargain on was that I needed them to know more than me to effectively do their jobs on the team and it worked out to my advantage to pass certain tasks over to those who thought they could do them. Although the meeting started with me being sure that every team members was looking critically in my direction, by the end of the meeting, when they knew that I depended upon them for their expertise, they didn't feel as hostile and didn't actually mind that all I was there to do was to put their heads together to create solutions. I even told them how needed they were and that I had the tedious job of reporting back and that endeared me to them a little more, since none of them actually liked that part of the job, since they were "hands on" types of workers and were much happier actually being trusted to do the jobs that they were expert at. You can make your job a whole lot easier when you learn to communicate effectively and clearly. That's what team leadership is all about and you will be respected for it.

Alan Anderson

Chapter 12 – Learning the Art of Allocation/Delegation

One of the things that management has to do is allocate work to certain team members. The next chapter covers getting to know your team members, but if you are a good team leader, you will know that you can't hog the whole job yourself, just because you know how to do it. Allocation of work or the delegation of certain tasks is always hard for newcomers to team leadership. They want to oversee the job to perfection and thus don't want to trust important aspects of that work to people who work under them. There's a very good reason for this. They are afraid of failure.

The problem is that when you are new to running a team, you want to impress the people who are in charge of you and you can't do that if you cannot produce the desired results within the given timeframe. It's not at all unusual for people not to know how to delegate correctly, but as a team leader it is a skill that you are going to have to learn and learn fast. The job is the team's job – not yours. Thus, the people working within your team should each be given a share of that job, which makes up the whole job. Each of the people that takes a part of the job works within their particular field of expertise. That means that you need to know who they are. But delegation goes further than that. You are placing trust in team members an when you are new at being a team leader, that's one of the hardest things to do.

Talk to your team as is indicated in the next paragraph and get to know them, by all means, but look for something that is vital to success. Who is strong? Who can you trust? Make sure that the team is totally aware that when you give them a task, it's your job to trust them so it's equally their job to be trustworthy. Delegation is letting go. It trusts someone to do something for you and many bosses come unstuck because they don't have the first clue about how allocation/delegation should be done.

Delegation directions

When you delegate you give something to someone else to do. There are two directions you can delegate in – one being up to management and one being down to employees who hold a lesser position to you. Something may need more managerial input before you can deal with it. In this case, you would delegate it back to your boss and let your boss decide how that task gets dealt with. Once you have put the job back into the hands of the boss, your hands are no longer tied until he has made his decision. Another manner in which you use upward delegation is when one of your team has specialized knowledge in an area where you don't. This could mean that you delegate engineering jobs to an engineer, etc., but you are still overall responsible for the end result as the team leader. When you delegate something in a downward direction – you hand it to someone else to do. In this case, you free yourself up to advance your career, instead of making yourself a workhorse doing things that someone junior to you could easily be doing.

The Reason you need to Learn Delegation

Often people don't like asking other people to do things for them. However, as a team leader it's your job to do it. I once asked an employee I had put in charge of a team why she was doing mundane work. She replied that she would never ask a team member to do something that she was not prepared to do herself. I admired that answer, but then told her about why a team leader allocates work. They don't do it because they don't want to do the work. They do it because every member of the team is equally important and needs to have a role to play. If the team leader does everything, then the members of the team feel that they are not trusted to do that job. That's a bad signal to a team member. Instead of doing the job by herself, I explained that she should delegate the work and then always be around to congratulate and appreciate what that worker did, letting the worker know that she was appreciative and did know what was involved in the task. You stunt your own career when you cannot delegate. Your desk gets filled to brimming with things that are actually beneath or above your station and it stunts your own growth as a leader. That's not a very good position to be in when you have a project that needs doing. Learn to delegate as it helps to free up time for you to be doing more important things that can advance your career.

Delegating with clear instructions

When you allocate work to someone because their expertise is better than yours, you are still accountable for the results within the project that you are working on. Make sure that the instructions you give your staff are completely clear and that there is no room for doubt on completion dates, dates when reviewing the situation will happen and exactly what you expect that member of staff to achieve. Delegation is one of the first skills that management learn because it's vital to actually being able to manage other people, together with their skillsets and their abilities. Of course, a team leader has the right to want reports at certain stages or to be approached if a team member has difficulty, but the whole team needs to have specific jobs that all link together to help finish whatever the project is.

Delegation or allocation of work goes further than that too. It will determine your ability to advance in your career. It's basically handling people and if you are good at it, this works well to help you achieve a higher position later on. People handling isn't the most easy job for anyone to do, but when the boss sees that delegation comes naturally to you, that means that he is going to trust you with more and more responsibility and that's a good sign for your future.

Investment

All of the things that you teach each other within a team are an investment for a company. For example, in your team, you may actually learn skills through delegation. If someone on your team achieves wonderful results and you don't know how these were done, ask. It shows appreciation for your team member and it also shows you that the trust you placed in him/her was well founded. The employee feels very satisfied about the achievement and you invest long term in having him share his expertise with others in the team so that the team is more complete in their knowledge base. That really does make good sense.

When Virgin's Richard Branson talked on a website about entrepreneurs, he said that the teams that you choose to work with are paramount to your success. You choose teams that you trust. You give them the work to do because you trust them and that frees you up to do more. It makes very good sense that top management don't waste their time on tasks which are considered to be suitable for others whose qualifications are more suited to the task.

Thus delegation comes high on the list of skills that a team leader has to learn about. Don't give work out until you know who is capable of doing what, or you may have a struggle on your hands getting that part of the task back to give to someone else. Instead, learn the strength of the team as shown in the next chapter. Once you have learned to delegate, you will find that it comes more naturally. We are so accustomed to doing our work and minding out own business that when it comes to asking someone else to do something, it isn't that easy. You do need to learn this skill as a team leader and your boss obviously had confidence in your ability or you would not be in the position you were chosen for. Give it time. It takes a while to be comfortable with delegation but when you are, it frees up so much of your time. When you know your team member's strengths and weaknesses it becomes very clear which job should be given to which member of the team, but you have to do this in a way where other team members will not be upset by your choices. Make each team member's role within the team vital to the overall conclusion. That way, they won't feel slighted and you will have included all skillsets and levels into the success equation. That's your job as a team leader and it's vital that you do this.

Chapter 13 – Team Incentives

One of the reasons why people achieve in this world is that they love competition. They actually enjoy it and you can try offering your team incentives, even if these are not financial ones. I remember in one business where I worked, they used a chart to show the progress of each member of a team during a project. At the end of each day, the employee filled in a progress chart in the form of a graph on the wall of the office to show how far along they were with their part of the task.

Recognition is very important for people who are team members because that recognition makes their workday worthwhile. Imagine – You spend at least seven hours a day at work within the work environment. You go home tired and with thoughts of work in your head. You may even face traffic holdups on the way back home. During all of that time, you don't get any fun with family and friends, except perhaps a snatched lunch hour when work permits it and even that's a luxury in this day and age.

So how can you make projects more competitive?

The way that you do this is to bring the team together and tell them what you have to achieve. Once everyone has their place in the team and knows what their allotted jobs are, they can either work singularly or in a team of two or more on parts of the project. You can choose whether the team project is one where each member gets recognition or whether you want to pit one team against the other in a competition to try and meet or even beat deadlines.

Make a chart on the wall of the office and add the team names to the chart or the teams, giving them names such as blue team or red team. Tell them that at the end of each day, they are to fill in a piece of paper to tell you just how far along they are with their project but that they must not discuss this progress with other team members.

I found that this worked better than getting people to mark their progress on a chart on the wall because people tended to exaggerate their progress when they compared their progress with others. By filling out a form each night before going home, the teams can give a clear indication of how much of the job has been done in percentages. Thus, if they have four weeks to complete something and consider that it will only take three, they have already advanced and can write down the percentage of the task that has already been achieved.

It's important to let the whole team know that this isn't a contest for superiority. It's a fun in house contest to help the team to work together and to compete in a friendly manner. Perhaps you don't have a huge prize in mind but maybe you can come up with something in house that would be equally as fun. Perhaps having a trophy that is passed from team member to team member as the job progresses toward the end.

The boss fills out the wall chart every morning before anyone is permitted to see it. He can assess any progress that he is in doubt of and talk to employees about progress at any time, but the idea is that workers look forward to coming into work in the morning and looking to see how they are doing compared with the rest of the team. In team sports, people support each other and really do want to go home with the victory. Competition within a team works very well as well and gets people energized and ready to take on the challenge of a new day.

At any time during the contest or the project, if anyone feels that their progress is being hampered by having to wait for someone else to finish something, they can report this and the boss can check into it. This is just so that the competition is kept fair at all times. If you let team members know that the contest is only fun, they will probably be happy to participate – knowing that it makes the work load a little more fun to deal with and gives them incentives to work better as a team.

Management: Take Charge of Your Team

Half way through a challenge such as this, you can change team members if you want to, meaning that if you believe that someone else will show a better performance in a certain task, you can switch people. They will probably be happy to be switched, especially if their progress is looking painfully slow.

This also helps you to keep an eye on the whole project and be aware when any team member has a problem with their part of the project. Being aware is always important. If you have some part of the project to do yourself, join in and be part of the contest for the fun of it and let people see that you are willing to stand up and be counted too. That always drives people toward working in a more harmonious way. Team incentives are great for motivation and they also help you to see the fun side of your team. They will surprise you. They may even amaze you, but if you make it fun, they will also enjoy the process and so will you. That's how great team management happens and everyone will be working toward the same aims as great teams do.

Alan Anderson

Chapter 14 – Learning Conflict Resolution

When you put more than one person into a room, there can be conflict. Expect it and be ready for it. If you find that two or more members of your team are disagreeing on something, you need to resolve it because this will hold up results and cause lack of motivation. No one likes going into work knowing that there's a personality clash waiting for them, so you need to decide how to deal with the situation. Here are some alternatives:

- An open meeting with the whole team
- A meeting with the members of the team who disagree
- Changing roles of members so that clashing members don't work together

The last option really should be the last thing that you consider. If you don't want to involve others in the problems that are ensuing between two or more members of the team, then the best bet is to call the problematic members to a team meeting that excludes others who are not yet demotivated.

You do need to talk about the problems and let each member that has an argument speak in turn in order to tell you what the problem is from their point of view. Don't allow interruption and tell each member of the team that is present at the meeting that it's vital that each of you get the problem off your chest, so that you are in a position to do something to help the situation. Explain that personality problems or conflict problems do need to be brought to a head because it's affecting the team as a whole and is making everyone unhappy and less productive.

Listen to what your team members say. Perhaps they themselves have a great idea and feel that they are being held back because of what other members of the team have been asked to do.

Perhaps jobs overlap and it hasn't been made clear who should do which part of the job. Remember to point out to the team that you need honest answers as to what's going wrong, so that you can appraise the situation and do something about it and never be afraid to take a little of the blame yourself.

"Perhaps some of this is my fault for having jobs that overlap and we need to look at that."

"Perhaps we need to talk about changes that will help you all to be the most productive."

Remember that people who have conflict won't be very happy. You need to see what's wrong from every perspective. Although some team leaders do see everyone separately to assess conflicts, I always think that the most adult way to deal with these is to have everyone in the same room and be ready to address the problems that they have. In one team that I led, it seemed that two people needed access to one terminal and because of the concentrated nature of the task, the terminal was never free for employee B, because employee A had too much to do and needed to be on that terminal. That was my fault. I should have gaged the situation better and simply providing Member B with an alternative terminal helped the situation and mended the relationship between both team members. I explained how intense the research that Member A was doing was, so that Member B didn't carry on thinking that Member A was just being pedantic and difficult. They still work together today and occasionally have disputes, but nothing that impedes the flow of a job because they are more professional and know how to get around problems of that nature.

Management: Take Charge of Your Team

One of your jobs as a team leader is to lead and that means being able to step in and tell people when they are out of line. Be very sure of your footing when you do this, as there may be reasons. It's better to hear their side of the story before leaping in and making mistakes. One employee looked like they did very little toward a project but the fact was that others just made more noise about what they did. In fact, this member who didn't move from his desk throughout the project, was actually doing very important work behind the scenes but not making a great deal of fuss about it like the others. When I added up productive hours lost on the job, it wasn't the quiet guy that was responsible. It was those who made the most noise about the work they were doing, but who were actually producing less work than him.

Personalities are difficult to deal with sometimes but in one project that I ran, emotions were running far too high and team members were starting to get personal with each other. I closed the office door, I called everyone to the center of the room and I told the team that we were not leaving the room until tempers had been cleared up and the frustrations of members had been voiced. They actually did a very good job of demonstrating to each other how futile the whole dispute was and came away from the meeting feeling like they had been heard. That's important but it's also important to remember that the project is everything and that each of your team need to be giving it everything they have, rather than wasting time in personal squabbles. In this case, there was a lot of shouting done by certain members of the team, but bringing it to a head was probably the best move in the circumstances because it managed to get them all seeing the futility of all of their arguments, when compared with the importance of the job. Conflict resolution is something that can really show your skills as a leader. Never lose your temper. Never take sides. Always see the bigger picture and help your team to see it too. Once you side with a particular member of staff, you may lose the respect of others. Thus stay professional and neutral in order to work out the problems and find solutions.

Alan Anderson

Chapter 15 – Shifting Deadlines or Changed Projections

One experience you may learn first-hand isn't a very pleasant one. What happens when you work for a company is that there is a hierarchy. You have your boss, he has his boss, etc. and you lead your team who consider you to be their boss. Sounds straightforward, doesn't it? The problem is that sometimes it isn't that straightforward. Too many chiefs and not enough Indians is a common phrase in business that will rear its ugly head when you are a team leader.

Your boss gives you the project but what he doesn't know is that his boss promised results two weeks before his deadline. As days pass, and meetings are held between bosses, things can change and that can upset the whole applecart as far as your team is concerned. If you are called in and told of changes, keep your team informed. It's no good thinking about how you are going to tell them and putting it off. The longer you do that, the bigger the problem will be because your team may be working in a certain fashion and that work may be wasted if the boss changes the whole purpose of the project.

Be friendly with your team. Let them know when you know. Let them come up with ideas that help you to keep on track. If you know one particular team member has put in extra effort and that effort is going to be wasted because of changes to the project, make sure that you can make that member of your team feel valued and have some reason why the work that they have already produced will be useful for other things.

When you have a hierarchy of management, expect the unexpected. You can even warn the team in advance that changes may be made – knowing what your management are like at doing that – but that for the time being this is the project. They will probably already be aware of how things change in the business

Alan Anderson

but it's important that they are prepared. A changed deadline that means they have to work harder or a changed project conclusion that can mean work they have done already is wasted and can cause resentment.

Have you ever watched TV shows where different departments in a company seem to be working against each other? A good example is when you have programs about the FBI and the cops working together. Someone always seems to be fighting someone else, but what he or she actually wants to achieve is the same result. Make it clear to your team that there is always the possibility of changes in the schedule and that they should be prepared for this, especially if you know your management to be likely to implement changes.

If you do have a deadline and do what I told you previously – move it back so your team has less time to finish the project – chances are that you can salvage the situation. Your team will have been working toward finishing their work on the 15th when in fact you know the real deadline to be the 22nd. That gives you more time to sort out any messes that management make and any changes they expect your team to go along with during the course of the project.

Holding a meeting to announce changes

As soon as you know about changes that affect the work that your team are doing, tell them. It's no good doing it by memo because you could cause bad feelings to fester and remain unspoken. That makes your team a little suspicious of you and unhappy about what they have been told in an impersonal email.

If you can have management at the meeting to explain why changes are necessary, that will help you considerably, but usually management are too busy making changes to see the impact that it has on the workforce. If changes that are made have an impact on your team, tackle it in person with all team members present. The idea of this is because you are a team and your team members may be able to come up with ideas to help you to keep the project on track. Sometimes, a comment by a member of the team can spark an idea and the whole team gathers its enthusiasm again and leaves the meeting – not feeling that management are trampling all over them – but that they, as a team, managed to find solutions.

Team members may also be able to suggest changes in who does what if the end result of the project has changed and they think the game plan needs changing too. Putting your heads together to come up with solutions is better than burying your head in the same and being afraid to tackle your team in person. There are some times when email memos are not enough. This is one of them. Changing plans or changing deadlines affect everyone and you show respect to your workers by remembering that and including them in plans to get the project back on track with their help, rather than their resentment. If the team feel that you are part of it and that you understand their frustrations and are with them one hundred percent, you will get a better response from them and they will become more flexible in their approach to try and help you to achieve the impossible tasks that management sets you.

Alan Anderson

Chapter 16 – Reporting of Problems

During the course of a project, your team may find that they get resistance from other staff elsewhere in the business. For example, shop floor staff may not be too willing to share information with them. Research and development teams may think that your team is wasting their time when they ask questions that are important to the progress of the project.

The problem is that your team needs to be able to report this kind of problem to you straight away so that you can take this up with the appropriate department and explain the reasons why your team needs their cooperation. I remember one such project where the research and development team thought that as long as they kept within their own parameters, they were not actually answerable to anyone. I had to take this problem to management because it was making our project difficult to do. We needed facts and figures that only they had and they were putting all of our emails at the bottom of the pile because they didn't understand the urgency of the matter until it was explained.

The first thing to do as a team leader is to telephone those departments that appear to be giving your team problems and see if you can smooth the way yourself. If this proves to be impossible, write out exactly what you need from that department and take it higher, reassuring your team that all is being done that can be to try and get things running smoothly.

Suppliers

Often when you are on a team project, you need access to supplies. If suppliers are playing hard to get, then you really do need to find out what the delay is. Maybe you need to use alternative suppliers so that your team has everything that they need in a timely manner. There was a case like this on one project where all we were trying to do was come up with a mount that was suitable for an antenna. This was a seemingly small project but it played a part in a larger project. The part that we could not access when we needed it, or in time for our deadlines was a simple screw fixing that was sized to the antenna bracket. No one seemed to have any of these in stock.

Without making major adaptations which would have eaten a lot of time and expense, we managed to find a supplier that had exactly what was needed and had to go through the process of getting our buyer to agree to purchasing these items at the rate that they had quoted.

Remember whether it's suppliers or other staff that are causing potential delays, as a team leader, it's your job to smooth the way and make sure that everything is on time and that nothing is getting in the way of finishing the project on time. Clients may be depending upon it. Your company reputation may be depending upon it. Claw your way through the difficulties and let this be your problem rather than a problem and an obstacle for your team. They will respect you for having intervened and sorted out a potential delay factor.

Making your team aware

When you have your initial meeting with your team, make it clear that you are there to help them when obstacles arise and that instead of waiting for obstacles to clear on their own, to report in and tell you what needs to be done straight away, so that you, as the team leader, can action remedial activities to get the project back on course.

If you do a challenge, it is a good indication of your team's progress and if they have a particularly slow day, find out why. Your team members may have pent up frustrations that they have not aired and without knowing that information, there's not much you can do to help them. I learned a long time ago to exaggerate deadlines. If my boss has told me a project needs to be finished by the 22nd, my deadline will be the 15th. That means that I always have time to sort out hiccups that may put the deadline off course, as and when they happen and that's vital. As a team leader, you can do that and make sure that all members of the team let you know if anything is stopping them from meeting the deadline that you give them. I actually love team leading. I find that it forges great relationships and helps you to see the strengths and weaknesses of different individuals. Never think of one member as being dead wood. If they are, then you haven't got them in the right job. It's your responsibility as a team leader to ensure that every member is placed in a position within the team where their strengths are really put to the test. The young girl I had on my team who was more interested in her love life, was actually great at figure-work, so I put her onto the team that had to do calculations and she really did do well. However, had I put someone into that work who was not particularly adept with figures, this would have slowed down the whole process. Know your team. Appreciate their talents and celebrate their abilities and strengths but also know their weaknesses and be able to be on hand to help sort out problems as and when they occur.

Alan Anderson

Chapter 17 – Crises and How to Manage Them Efficiently

Crisis management is one of the toughest jobs a manager will have to perform. This is because crises don't' follow rules and regulations. They happen due to different circumstances and under different conditions that a manager can't claim expertise in handling the next one because it will be totally different from the other. As such, crises managers need to be very confident and quick on their feet when it comes to managing crises efficiently.

Throughout your training, you will have gone through the mundane routine so that it is what your brain will be accustomed to. It takes a certain type of test of leadership skill in order to perform well in a crisis.

Hence, it is very crucial that in order to prove yourself, you know exactly how to handle any crisis that may arise in your path to becoming an effective and efficient manager.

Here is a list of characteristics you need to remember that will help you deal with any and all sorts of crises:

- **Be Critical and Realistic:** As a manager, you are the leader and a leader is never found at the back of the crowd. He is at the front line, leading his team forward. Hence, you should always deal with a crisis head-on. This will inspire the members of your team to keep calm and perform well under crises too.

This is possible only if you clear any and all illusions you have about the crisis. Gather as much facts and information about the crises being experienced because only through these will you be able to sift the illusions from reality, the myths from certainties.

As you gather such facts and information and sift away the illusions about the crisis, critically analyze all the points of your crisis and plan your strategy according to that. Otherwise, you'll fail to contain the crisis and may let it escalate even further. Don't just go all gung-ho with no solid plan of action, simply hoping for the results to work out. Create a foolproof plan based on the information and facts you gathered so that you won't have to rely on luck for your success.

- **Strategy and Detail:** As a manager, your strategy matters most. You need to see the problem and then look at it from a bigger picture – see the forest and not the trees as Stephen Covey once wrote. A good and effective manager knows both what is at the top of the mountain and at the base of it. Hence, your vision should be all encompassing.

You also need to look at the wave and see the ripples it will cause – know the cause and all possible repercussions of your alternative courses of action as much as possible. True, you can't perfectly predict all the possible results of a course of action but that shouldn't stop you from exhausting all possible ideas. If you don't, you run the risk of pouring gasoline over the crisis flame and escalate it even further.

Even if you haven't ever faced a crisis of this sort before, you should accept the fact that regardless of your inexperience of such a crisis, you're the one who will need to solve it and thus you should take courage and the lead in managing it. The buck stops with you as the manager and you can't resort to blaming when things go down.

This will mean getting down into the fray and learning all there is to learn about it. Get information about your crisis and think about how you can untangle this knot of problems. Remember that your problem will only get solved with minimal damage if you know what cause and effect is. Hence, make a plan of what you are to do and what result that will cause. Thus, your crisis will seem small and you will be able to handle anything easily.

- **Weigh Your Options:** As a manager, you know by now that there are two sides to everything but when it comes to crises, there are more than 2 sides to consider. Know that there will be many ways to handle a crisis but you need to handle it gracefully so that you handle it quickly, efficiently and without damage to your own goals. Choosing how you handle it without careful thought is the single biggest obstacle to your being able to contain it fast and well.

This might mean that you will have to consult with your own team and others as well. Never be afraid to ask for advice, there's no shame in doing so. The real shame is when you screw up and escalate the crisis even more because you were too proud to ask for help. Ask even if this means that you have to go and talk to other managers like yourself, educate yourself on a crisis and ask for advice.

Though at the end you might want to follow your initial plan and do what you wanted to in the beginning, you will have a very clearer view of what you are doing and change plans accordingly if needed. As you do, you'll avoid worrying about whether or not you could've handled it better. This is extremely crucial for your own peace of mind since a crisis will stress you out in a great way so you need to eliminate all doubts from your system. Confidence in your ability to take control and peace of mind is key here.

- **Make Decisions:** Take this as an extension of the last point but you will have to make decisions and make them at the right time. There is nothing worse in a crisis than a wrongly timed decision because a right decision made a second too late is still a wrong one.

To make a decision, you will have to listen to your gut and take the decision that you honestly know and believe to be the best alternative. This only comes after years upon years of experience. A new manager cannot take the best decision because they will always be indecisive due to his or her relative inexperience in handling crises. Hence, here is the time when you need to call upon all your years of training and find any instances where you dealt with or saw someone dealing with some crisis of the similar sort if you are new to managing crises or at being a manager in general.

Decision making, however, is not simply setting things in motion. You also need to sell the decision to other people that are critical to successfully handling a crisis such as your superiors and to some extent, your subordinates who'll be carrying out your decision. If you don't, you run the risk of failing to get their full support, which may prove to be the undoing of your crisis management plan of action.

Make a decision, detail WHY you took that particular decision and also enlist the results this decision will cause. Try to pick a decision that will cause the least amount of damage possible. Then, go in with full confidence in your choice. Remember that in the end, it all comes down to rational and realistic thinking and hence any decision based on this is the decision that is best. The clearer you're able to present your case and the more confident you are in them, the greater are your chances of winning their support.

- **Collaborate:** Like we mentioned before, never be afraid to ask advice of anyone. If making the best decision means asking help from team-member or another manager, do it. Remember, humility is as important a character trait of an effective manager as is confidence. In fact, it takes a lot of confidence to be humble enough and ask for other people's help.

Be very clear of your goals, which are to reach a particular point. And if you think that someone can help you reach your goal in good time and in a better way, ask for help. You won't regret doing so, especially if it leads to your being able to successfully resolve or manage a crisis.

Collaboration can mean both working with your team, a particular team-member that you feel can help you in this specific time of need or another manager who might have more experience or experience in a similar way. It doesn't matter if the person or people you collaborate with are from your team or outside of it. What matters is you collaborate with people who'll be able to help successfully handle crises.

Work on the principle that two heads are better than one and if nothing else, you will have another set of eyes to view the problem from. You have blind spots, as with everyone else and having another set of eyes can help you see these blind spots and enable you to manage crises much better. This means that perhaps your decision might be improved or you might find a much easier solution to your problem, both of which will be in your favor.

Collaboration will also help you to beat stress since a second opinion can help you see that your problem might not be as big as you imagined and this will help you reach a conclusion in a better way. Many times, we feel overwhelmed with certain situations because we are either too close to the problem or inside it. The opinion of someone who's detached from the situation can help assure you that the crisis you're handling may not be as big as you thought it is.

- **Take Note Of Adverse Opinion:** Remember how we

talked about the value of conflicts or differing opinions and preferences within a team? A bad and inefficient manager is one who only surrounds him or herself with those who agree with them because these people either have the same blind spots as him or herself or people with no convictions. Such people are easily pressured into making wrong decisions or acting unwisely and are thus practically worthless to the manager.

If you love surrounding yourself with people whom always - or most of the time - agree with you, beware. This might make you feel good in the short term but in the long run, you will find yourself in a very lonely position indeed. This means that since you will only find people who agree with everything you say, you will always have to make decisions yourself and you will only have your own opinion reflected back at you. You're not able to enjoy the benefit of being able to really see things as they are and act or decide accordingly. You're at high risk of bungling crises or fail to even manage your team well even if there're no crises.

Avoid this. Heed the advice to "keep your enemies closer". Keep your critics close because they will show you where you are wrong and this will help you improve greatly. You will never be one hundred percent effective but you always need to strive for that extra ten percent. This means listening to everyone who criticizes you.

Keep in mind that not every critic will be accurate, however. Some people will try to bring you down most deliberately. These are not your friends, either. This is where a good confidence in your own abilities and judgments will come into play. When you're aware of your own capabilities as well as limits, you'll be in a great position to determine the true value of your critics' opinions about you and your courses of action.

As such, take every advice and analyze it critically so you neither miss something important nor grow insecure because of the gossip or language of others. The goal is to get accurate feedback that will help you become an even more effective manager or leader.

- **Stay Calm and Positive:** Being critical is the first step and it is a most important one. However, never let yourself grow pessimistic because even if they seem similar, being critical and pessimist are two different things. Being critical is simply trying to identify all things that can possibly go wrong with the intention of being able to address them should they happen while being pessimist is simply believing more in the negative side of things without the intention of eventually addressing them.

Whilst in a crisis, you are the leader and your team will be looking up to you. If you get too critical, there is a great chance you will grow increasingly pessimistic. This will cause you to grow depressed which will sap your energy. But not only this, such a habit will affect your team as well.

That's why a much as critical thinking is important when handling crises, you shouldn't go overboard. Be very sensitive to your team members' reactions to see if you're overdoing it because your team will be, especially in the case of a crisis, monitoring and copying your every move. If you go into the ordeal head-on, they will be courageous too. If you remain calm, they will feel like everything is under control. However, the slightest sign of trouble and their morale will start to wane and decrease as well. Hence you'll need to also rein in your critical thinking to prevent pessimism.

Stay calm – or at least pretend to be so – and you will eventually clear your own head and will be able to look at the crisis in a much better way than you had been before. Hence, even when it feels like the walls are caving in, keep a level head and find your nearest and safest exit and you will make it. Just continue holding the fort while in the midst of crises.

- **Take Risks:** Timely decisions are wonderful but the reality is it involves risk, which is defined as the chance of something unfavorable happening. You can't eliminate risk – you can only manage it either by doing things that will lower the chances of it materializing or preparing to manage its potential effects should materialize. A crisis is a crisis only because you have not dealt with it previously. Thus, it's alright to be afraid. However, be rational about your fear, which is only based on the fact that you have not been there before. Eventually, your mind will reassure itself about your ability to handle a crisis because even though you haven't experienced the same kind before, you have been in other crises that you've managed well.

Hence, take risks and deliver yourself from this problem. Test waters before you jump in but when the results arrive, make haste in jumping in so that you may reach the results you desire.

As the economic rule goes, greater the risk, greater the profit. As such, you will need to plan out just exactly what it is that you are attempting to do if you want a bigger payoff. But when you do take that decision, give it your hundred percent because anything less significantly increases the possibility of associated risks materializing.

- **Choose The Safest Option:** This might seem easier said than done but in fact, it is one of the best ways of dealing with a crisis. To do this, you will need to clear your mind of any and all sorts of apprehensions.

How can you do this? By taking a break, turning off your cell phone and just writing down whatever options you have. Get away from any and all distractions so you can create a mini feasibility report and see which option causes the least damage whilst giving the best result in the most objective way you can. Distractions, especially those related to the crises you're handling, have a way of making people decide with much bias.

The objective you identify and evaluate your options, the higher your risk of failing to manage crises well. It's because some options might seem to give a hundred percent result but the damage would be great too and a clouded or biased judgment is usually unable to see those possible damages.

Avoid this. Remember that you need to play it safe. Pick the option with the lowest risk such as a result that might give an 80% of the result but only 5% damage as compared to 95% chances of success but with a possible damage of 20%. Ratios can be very handy when making such decisions because these are based on numbers (read: objective) and give you a clearer picture of what you are gaining and what you are losing.

However, when you do end up making a decision, stick to it and implement each and every aspect of it without doubting yourself. Remember that the time to hesitate has long since passed and therefore what you have is only what you have and you should utilize it to a hundred percent.

- **Admit Mistakes:** Remember that you are human. You will make mistakes. Don't demonize these and fear them to death. You can choose to look at mistakes as learning opportunities. I don't know with you but I believe mistakes are better teachers than the things we do right. With every crisis that you face, you will learn and get better. Hence, don't try to hide your mistakes; even if you make one, it is a crucial part of learning. Embrace them but don't long for and go after them. Do your best to avoid them and if you can't, simply take in the valuable lessons associated with them by asking empowering questions such as "How can I do things better to avoid making the same mistake in the future?" Hence, as soon as you realize your fault, correct it and move on to the next step of crisis management.

At the end, remember that no matter what happens, you will

never possess all ten of these characteristics right away. There will be a few points that will elude you for a long time until managing a crisis becomes as natural as making a cup of coffee. Also, with every crisis, you will learn more about handling the crises that are to come. Remember, practice doesn't necessarily make perfect but it can lead to mastery and excellence. The more you accept the fact that you can make mistakes along the way, the more you'll be able to make more effective decisions and learn from inevitable mistakes much better.

There's a lot of debate as to whether leaders are made or born. A lot of leaders possess these characteristics naturally and that is what makes them leaders. But there are a lot of people who never exhibited such traits in their childhood and even early adult years but because of circumstances or purposeful learning, they eventually learned how to become great leaders. Hence, if you aren't afraid to take risks and are willing to deal with anything head-on, you will be a master of these characteristics and more in record time even if you think you're not a naturally gifted leader. Hence, the one characteristic you need to possess in the largest quantity is that of courage because a great and efficient manager is one who is not afraid to take risks and lead his team through even the choppiest waters to get things done.

Conclusion

Team management is important, but it isn't about **being** important. It's about being there for your team members when they need you and overseeing the project from a managerial point of view. That means that you need to have a lot of skills including the ones shown in this book. Your team can only be as effective as you are. There is nowhere to throw blame when you are a team manager because the buck rests with you. However, when you do succeed as a team manager or leader, what you find is that your team members will follow your lead and will do so with added enthusiasm if they see that you have enthusiasm and vision to get a job done.

Listening skills and talking skills are also important to the task. You can't expect someone to have any kind of respect for you if that respect is not returned. Thus, learn to listen and remember that a project may be done more efficiently by using your own ideas and your team's combined ideas. Always give them credit for their ideas and work together, having mutual trust in your team. There are always jobs which are easier to do than others and you can place each member of the team into a strategic position which makes the most of their skills and that minimizes the risks that may be associated with their weaknesses.

Strong leaders or entrepreneurs such as Richard Branson trust their own judgment in appointing leaders because they know that the growth of their business depends upon it. If you have been appointed as a team leader, then your boss has recognized something in you that merits giving you that chance. By listening to your team and working closely with them, you can achieve great things. You may even finish your project before the set scheduled date if you all work together and you pick the right members of the team for the right jobs.

Alan Anderson

However, remember that scheduling meetings that are held to see if a project is on target is also essential and gives you a chance to re-appraise your choices. Flexibility, at the end of the day, is one of the most important attributes of a great leader. Add to that the vision to see the job through and to know what the target results should be and you, as a team leader, have a great chance to show your skills in the face of difficulty. It isn't the easiest job to have as when you put people together, things can fall apart. However by being in control of the whole project and the people working on it, you will learn who you can trust to be left to get on with their work and which members of the team need more coaching. Your skills at communication, coaching, problem resolving and being flexible in the face of difficulty are all part and parcel of your job as a team leader.

Finally, I'd like to ask you a favor if I may. If you enjoyed this book, then I'd really appreciate you leaving a review and your feedback on Amazon.

Thank you and good luck!

Printed in Great Britain
by Amazon